I'm full of Love!

Ruth's Self-discovery of Love

Published by LoveWorld Publishing Limited
3, Adebayo Akande Street, Oregun,
Ikeja, Lagos, Nigeria.
E-mail: info@loveworldbooks.org, info@kiddiesloveworld.org
Website: www.loveworldpublishing.org
ISBN 978-1-946026-30-9
Copyright © 2019 by LoveWorld Publishing.

Scripture taken from the New King James Version®.
Copyright © 1982 by Thomas Nelson, Inc. Used by permission. All rights reserved.

FOR MORE INFORMATION AND TO PLACE ORDERS:

UNITED KINGDOM:
LoveWorld
Unit C2, Thames View Business Center,
Barlow Way Rainham-Essex,
RM 13 8BT
Tel.: +44 (0) 1708 556 604
Fax: + 44 (0) 2081 816 290

USA:
LoveWorld
4237 Raleigh Street
Charlotte, NC 28213
Tel.: +1 980-219-5150

USA:
Christ Embassy Houston,
8623 Hemlock Hill Drive
Houston, Texas. 77083
Tel.: +1-281-759-5111
*   +1-281-759-6218*

CANADA:
4101 Steeles Ave W,
Suite 204 , Toronto, Ontario,
Canada M3N 1V7

SOUTH AFRICA:
303 Pretoria Avenue
Cnr. Harley and Braam Fischer,
Randburg, Gauteng
South Africa.
Tel.: +27 11 326 0971,
Fax: +27 113260972

NIGERIA:
Plot 97 Durumi District, Abuja,
Nigeria.

Kudirat Abiola Way, Oregun
P.O. Box 13563 Ikeja, Lagos.
Tel.: +234-812-340-6547
*   +234-812-340-6791*

"Whoever has this world's goods, and sees his brother in need, and shuts up his heart from him, how does the love of God abide in him? My little children, let us not love in word or in tongue, but in deed and in truth"

(1 John 3:17-18).

One day, Cindy invited her friend, Ruth to accompany her to deliver some groceries for her mom. It was Ruth's first time to visit in this other part of the city.

As usual, the streets were busy. Everyone seemed to be in a hurry, either going or coming from somewhere. Groceries and fruits were displayed for sale in the open, with little regard for hygiene.

Ruth could hardly believe what she saw. The streets were dirty and littered with waste spilling out from the garbage cans. The air seemed choked with the stench of rotten food.

Ruth held her nose tight with her fingers, to keep the smell away.

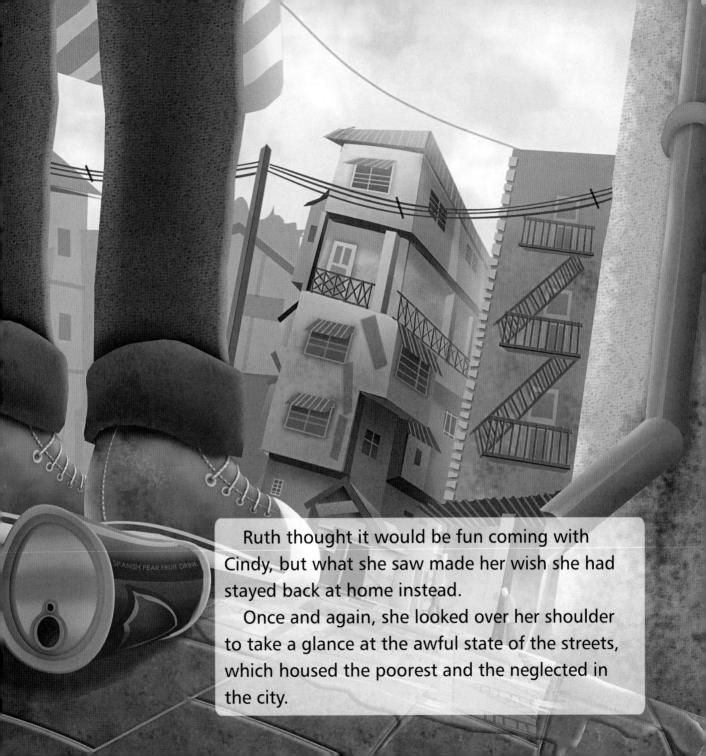

Ruth thought it would be fun coming with Cindy, but what she saw made her wish she had stayed back at home instead.

Once and again, she looked over her shoulder to take a glance at the awful state of the streets, which housed the poorest and the neglected in the city.

They walked through the streets, chatting and sometimes teasing at each other.

"This place looks disgusting," Ruth remarked with a frown. "Do people really live here?"

"Of course," Cindy replied; she saw a little boy across the street and smiled at him.

"Hey, why's that boy staring at me," Ruth said. "Doesn't he know it's rude to stare at people that way?"

"Come on, Ruth!" Cindy replied. "He's only a little boy. Besides, he hasn't seen you in this neighbourhood before."

"You know him?" Ruth asked.

Cindy chuckled. "Yes, I do, his name is Josh. Would you like to say hello to him?"

"I possibly can't do that," Ruth retorted. "I could be infected with germs if I got too close to him."

"You shouldn't talk that way as a Christian, Ruth," Cindy corrected.

"I know!" Ruth protested. "I'm just being careful."

They walked some distance and got to an old building that looked abandoned.

"Here we are!" Cindy said with much excitement. "This is where I'm delivering the groceries."

'What! Here? Oh gosh," said Ruth with displeasure.

Cindy smiled, "It's not as bad as you think. The people here are quite nice and warm."

"You mean, you know the people here, too?" Ruth asked.

"Yup! My mom discovered this place some weeks ago, and saw the folks here didn't have much to take care of themselves," Cindy replied. "Every week she brought food and clothes to them. So, I'm helping her out this week, because she had to attend to some other pressing issues."

"Let's go in," Cindy said to Ruth encouragingly. "You'd love them. They're kind."

"Love? How could I possibly love the people I've never met?" Ruth said, still upset with herself for coming. "It's a huge mistake to have come with you."

"Don't say that! You can love anyone," Cindy said. "Remember the story of the Samaritan in the Bible, who showed kindness to a man he'd never known.'

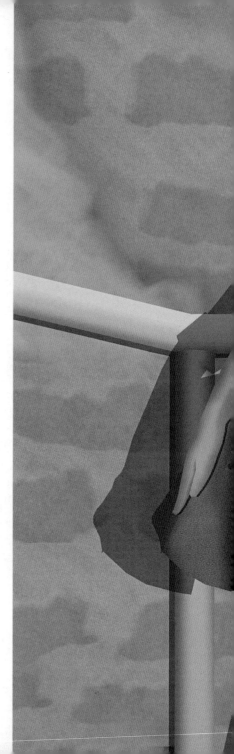

Ruth remembered the story Cindy was talking about. It was taught in her Sunday School few weeks back.

She could still recall how the wounded man laid helpless on the road after he was attacked by thieves.

A priest passed by, but didn't stop to help him.

A Levite also passed by, but just like the priest, he didn't stop to help the wounded man either.

Then a Samaritan came by that route too. When he saw the wounded man he had compassion on him, and hurried to his side. He cleaned his wounds and wrapped him with a bandage.

Then he took him to the inn, and paid the innkeeper to take care of him.

"Ruth, Ruth, Ruth!" Cindy called out as she waved her hands at Ruth to get her attention.

"Huh?" Ruth blinked. "Oh! I was thinking about the story of the good Samaritan."

"I thought as much," said Cindy.

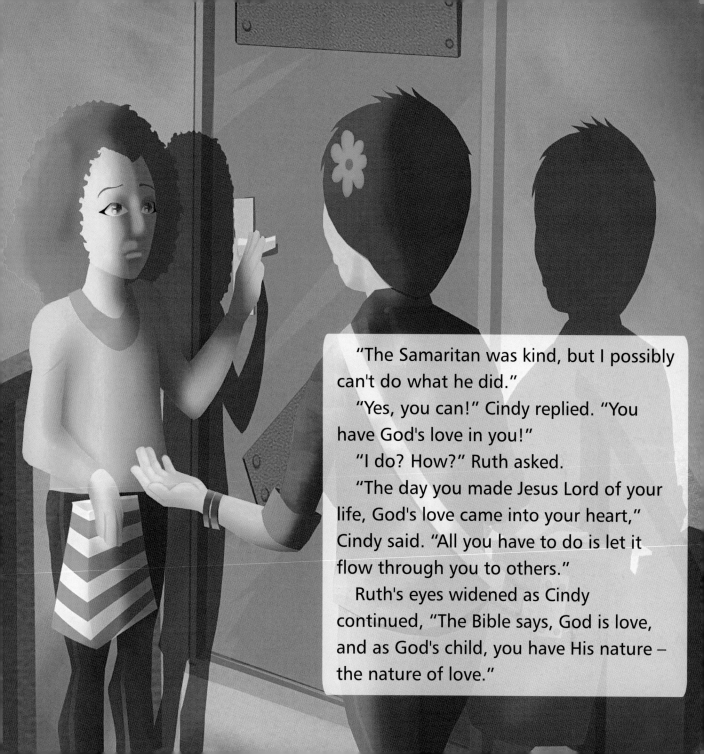

"The Samaritan was kind, but I possibly can't do what he did."

"Yes, you can!" Cindy replied. "You have God's love in you!"

"I do? How?" Ruth asked.

"The day you made Jesus Lord of your life, God's love came into your heart," Cindy said. "All you have to do is let it flow through you to others."

Ruth's eyes widened as Cindy continued, "The Bible says, God is love, and as God's child, you have His nature – the nature of love."

"You mean I have God's love too?" Ruth asked.

"YES!" Cindy giggled. "All you need do is ask the Holy Spirit to help you show it, and He will."

Cindy placed her arm across Ruth's shoulder and smiled. "Come on, I'd like you to meet these people," Cindy said to her friend.

Ruth smiled back at her and said, "Ok."

She held Cindy's hand tightly, and they walked to the door.

Cindy knocked on the wooden door, and almost immediately, someone answered. As the door swung open, a plain old lady with kind eyes appeared at the doorway.

"Aahh! Cindy!" Ms. Woods said with a spark on her face, and gave her a big hug.

"Hello Ms. Woods," greeted Cindy happily. "I came with my friend, Ruth."

Ms. Woods held her hands out to Ruth and said, "I'm glad you could come with Cindy."

Ruth didn't move. She stared at Ms. Woods, not knowing what to say. Cindy nudged her to respond.

'Er... thanks,' said Ruth, a bit hesitant.

Ms. Woods was excited the children paid her a visit. She welcomed them and asked them in.

"Come inside," she said. "Everyone will be very delighted to see you."

Ruth and Cindy stepped in, and Ms. Woods gently shut the door.

That day, Ruth and Cindy had a wonderful time with Ms. Woods and her family. They ate together and talked about different things.

Ruth also had a great time playing with the kids.

Ruth and Cindy helped Ms. Woods do the dishes in the kitchen; and also tidy up the house.

When they were done, it didn't matter to Ruth anymore how Ms. Woods' family looked or where they lived; she was glad she could love them, and help out in her own little way.

It was time for the girls to go home. They said goodbye to Ms. Woods and her family.

As they walked home, Ruth was glad she could let the love of Christ flow through her. She knew from that moment on she could love anybody.

"I didn't know I could allow God's love flow through me to Ms. Woods and her family," Ruth said to Cindy, with a smile.

"I'm glad you did," Cindy replied. "Jesus wants us to build a happier world with love."

"I'm all out for it," Ruth said excitedly.

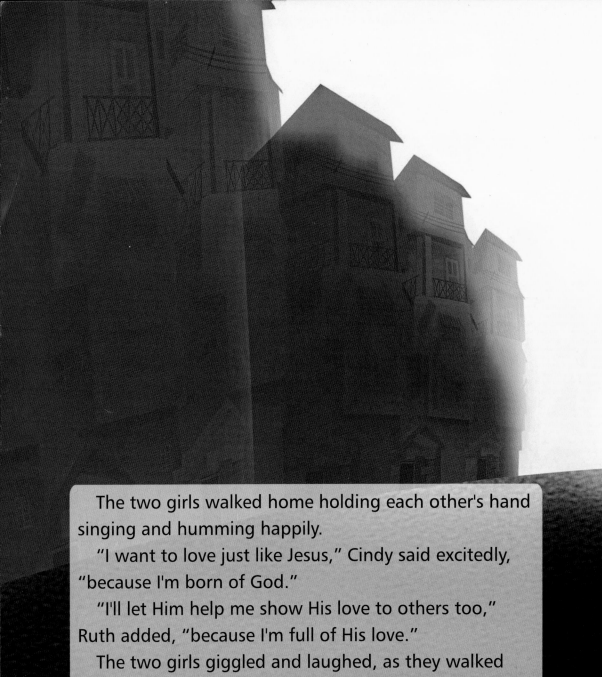

The two girls walked home holding each other's hand singing and humming happily.

"I want to love just like Jesus," Cindy said excitedly, "because I'm born of God."

"I'll let Him help me show His love to others too," Ruth added, "because I'm full of His love."

The two girls giggled and laughed, as they walked back home.

What The Bible Says

Below are some Scripture verses that talk about how to love others. Read them and memorise them.

(All Bible verses are from the New King James Version except where another version is indicated.)

1. "... the love of God has been poured out in our hearts by the Holy Spirit who was given to us" (Romans 5: 5).

2. "Let all that you do be done with love" (1 Corinthians 16:14).

3. "Beloved, let us love one another, for love is of God; and everyone who loves is born of God and knows God" (1 John 4:7).

4. "Most important of all, you must sincerely love each other..." (1 Peter 4:8 CEV).

5. "... love one another as I have loved you" (John 15:12)

6. "But I tell you to love your enemies and pray for anyone who mistreats you" (Matthew 5:44 CEV).

7. "Children, you show love for others by truly helping them, and not merely by talking about it" (1 John 3:18 CEV)

A Lesson For You

God wants you to show love to everyone you meet. He wants you to care for other people without expecting anything in return. And there are different ways to do so:

- You could share your meal with someone who has nothing to eat.

- You could give one or two of your nice clothes to someone in need of them.

- You could pray for a sick friend.

- You could become friends with the boy or girl in your class who is too shy to play with others.

- You could visit the elderly at the 'old people's home'.

- Get a gift for someone on his or her birthday.

- Say some nice words to someone who's discouraged.

These are just a few ways to show love to others; there are lots more.

What you need to do is to talk with the Holy Spirit, and ask Him to guide you.

And He sure will!

6 Great books to Have!

Children can live victoriously every day once they know what they've got inside them. Help them discover who they really are in Christ with these interesting story books from the "I Know Who I Am Collection", and watch them grow to become who God intended them to be.

I'm Different — Chris Oyakhilome

I'M BOLD — Chris Oyakhilome

I am Special — Chris Oya...

I'm Smart

I'm Beautiful — Chris Oyakhilome

I'm Full of Love — Chris Oyakhilome

To Order: **Call: NIG:** +234-812-340-6547; +234-812-340-6791
UK: +44 (0) 1708 556 604, **SA:** +27 11 326 0971
USA: +1 980-219-5150, +1-281-759-5111; +1-281-759-6218
Or send E-mail: info@loveworldbooks.org, info@kiddiesloveworld.org
Visit Website: www.loveworldpublishing.org

CHILDREN'S BOOKS